17 Highly-Guarded Strategies to Close Every Sale Guaranteed Plus How to Combat the Fear of Closing

John Di Lemme

17 Highly-Guarded Strategies to Close (Open) Every Sale
Guaranteed Plus How to Combat the Fear of Closing © 2008
John Di Lemme

Di Lemme Development Group, Inc.

931 Village Boulevard

Suite 905-366

West Palm Beach, Florida 33409-1939

877-277-3339

www.ChampionsLiveFree.com

This book is designed to provide competent and reliable
information regarding the subject matters covered. However,
it is sold with the understanding that the author is not engaged
in rendering legal, financial, or other professional advice.
Laws and practices often vary from state to state and if legal
or other expert assistance is required, the services of a
professional should be sought. The author specifically
disclaims any liability that is incurred from the use and/or
application of the contents of this book.

ISBN: 978-0-557-03078-1

Introduction

Seventeen highly guarded strategies to close every sale guaranteed! I have to admit, that's a powerful title for a book and full of a lot of action. I'm going to share with you seventeen specific highly guarded strategies to close every sale guaranteed. Now, I know that you're saying, "John, how can you guarantee it?" That's a great question especially since there are so many so-called coaches out there that "guarantee" everything and follow through on nothing.

Based upon my experience in sales, I have a very high closing ratio because I have a different kind of mindset than most people who teach sales and closing, and you're going to learn that. I suggest that you sit back, enjoy, and get ready for some serious revelations. Get ready to say to yourself, "Wow, I can't believe I never knew that. That's what's holding me back from closing my sales!"

This is just for champions! Only continue reading if you want to double your closing ratio and close every sale. I'm going

Are You a Member of the Fastest Growing Success & Motivation Club?
Check It Out Now! – www.LifestyleFreedomClub.com
17 Highly Controversial Motivational Teachings FREE ($497 value)

to share highly guarded strategies of the top closers in the world. I am one of them, and I challenge you to join the team of the champion closers. Also, if this is your first time reading this program, you have to review it six more times before you truly understand the empowering wisdom I'm going to share with you. It will take seven times until you chip away at all the useless garbage that you've been taught in the past that simply doesn't work. That's why most people in sales fail. Ninety-seven percent of people in sales are failing miserably. Do the complete opposite of what they're doing and you're going to succeed.

You see the word highly guarded, stands for to protect, watch over and keep confined. Most six and seven figure earners in sales will NEVER divulge their protected strategies to their competition. Remember, I'm your coach and want to see you succeed so I'm going to share the highly guarded strategies that I have used and am using right now to break all records in sales. I'm excited to share with you!

Are You a Member of the Fastest Growing Success & Motivation Club?
Check It Out Now! - www.LifestyleFreedomClub.com
17 Highly Controversial Motivational Teachings FREE ($497 value)

Strategies defined in the dictionary means a specific systematic plan of action for obtaining a specific goal or result. The general public...the general salesperson does not know these strategies. They may hear them but they won't adapt them, because 97% of salespeople do not make six figures a year. They simply can't think big enough to implement these life-changing strategies! It's really a shame, because the industry of sales is a great opportunity to earn huge income and live the life that you've always dreamed of living.

That's why I know you're reading this. You want something more! Acknowledge yourself. Pat yourself on the back, because today you're taking a major step in your sales career, your life and your career. The strategies that you learn in this material will give you that edge that you've been looking for all these years. You will surpass all of your competitors that just sit around doing the same old thing producing the same old results.

Close means have no openings. That means when you

Are You a Member of the Fastest Growing Success & Motivation Club?
Check It Out Now! – www.LifestyleFreedomClub.com
17 Highly Controversial Motivational Teachings FREE ($497 value)

go into a sales presentation, you leave with no openings, no chance of that person not becoming a client, customer, consultant, representative, or whatever your "end result" is to be. It's to close every sale. That's awesome. Isn't it? Write that down: I will close every sale, guaranteed! Now, I want you to keep that little affirmation somewhere so you see it everyday and believe that you can truly close every single sale.

Every sale? Do you really know what sale means to you and your business? In the dictionary, sale is defined as the transfer of ownership of property from one person to another in return for money. My mission through this book is for you to transfer the ownership of the property that you're marketing or selling to the individual that's in front of you. These strategies will work for everyone! It doesn't matter if you sell real estate, insurance, clothes or you are involved in Network Marketing. Let me repeat myself...these strategies will work for everyone reading this material! Whatever product you have, you want to transfer it to the customer, but it doesn't stop there. You want

Are You a Member of the Fastest Growing Success & Motivation Club?
Check It Out Now! – www.LifestyleFreedomClub.com
17 Highly Controversial Motivational Teachings FREE ($497 value)

them to remain your customer long-term. It's not a one time deal. It's longevity that builds a successful business.

Let's go over the word guaranteed. It's an agreement by which one person undertakes to secure another in the possession or enjoyment of something. I am going to guarantee that after you read this material you will possess the skills to explode your results in sales and marketing. Here's the catch...You can't just read the strategies and expect for them in some way to attract success for you. It's action not attraction that yields success in any business! You have to take action and implement these strategies into your business.

The number on reason why people earn huge income is because they are closers! But like I said before, you don't just close a sale and then you're done. Anyone that teaches that is completely wrong. Closing is actually opening up relationships. When one door closes, another one opens. You are continually opening doors of opportunity through your closing skills when you maintain those long-term relationships

Are You a Member of the Fastest Growing Success & Motivation Club?
Check It Out Now! - www.LifestyleFreedomClub.com
17 Highly Controversial Motivational Teachings FREE ($497 value)

with the customers that you have moved through the process.

Closing isn't second nature to most people and can be a little intimidating at first. Through these strategies, I am literally going to bulletproof your belief in yourself and your ability to close. Fear won't stand a chance. I am going to teach you exactly how to achieve more success, overcome the fear of closing, and beat the apprehension that builds when you think about doing a sale. The bottom line is: You are going to get focused! You are going to get very clear on what you need to do in order to develop and build your lifestyle and business.

WARNING: This isn't going to be popular with 99% of the world, but I don't care about them. I care about you. Believe in what you are going to learn in this book, and understand that the art of closing will absolutely put an end to frustration in your sales and marketing business.

Strategy #1: The Fear of Closing

You have to combat the fear of closing to overcome that obstacle. You can't even move forward in the sales process until you have conquered this fear. The underlying fear of closing is the fear of success. Your mind is saying is, "What if I actually create a relationship with the person, open up a relationship, develop a bond with the person, and they trust me to do business. All of a sudden, I've got the right to close the sale and earn that 6% commission." Let's say 6% of $1,000,000 is $60,000.00. You have never earned that before so your internal belief structure is full of fear. Not only is that a lot of money, but the responsibility that goes along with it and the dedication to the client is terrifying for most people.

You must self-develop and stretch yourself. I have seen so many people that have a great product, have a great service, and they have an absolute right to earn huge income, but they have a fear of closing. They simply don't believe in themselves enough to take a step of faith and just do it. The

Are You a Member of the Fastest Growing Success & Motivation Club?
Check It Out Now! – www.LifestyleFreedomClub.com
17 Highly Controversial Motivational Teachings FREE ($497 value)

only way to combat that underlying fear of closing that is holding you back is to get totally immersed in self-development. I've never met a person that invests time in personal development material that is completely shell-shocked at the thought of closing. Why? Because their belief in their own abilities and their business vehicle outweighs that fear.

Don't even think about giving me the excuse that you don't have time or the money to invest in success and motivation. It's literally minutes and pennies a day! Isn't your success worth that? If you don't know where to start, then become a member of our Lifestyle Freedom Club where you have the ability to immerse yourself in personal development 24 hours a day, 7 days a week. We bombard you with incredible information that allows you to build a solid foundation of self-belief. You see, I love to close. Why? Because I know that I am opening long-term relationships with people that want to succeed. Print this out, circle this, and

Are You a Member of the Fastest Growing Success & Motivation Club?
Check It Out Now! – www.LifestyleFreedomClub.com
17 Highly Controversial Motivational Teachings FREE ($497 value)

put it in front of you: "I love to close, because I am opening up a long-term relationship."

Like I said before...When one door closes, another one opens. Isn't it amazing to know that every time you close a sale, you open a door of opportunity not only for that customer but also yourself. You must internalize that opportunity and look forward to closing the sale so that you can open those life-changing doors.

I am under the assumption that you are marketing an ethical and moral product. When you have an ethical and moral product that will change someone's life, then you have a right to earn huge income through that product. You notice that I did not say "make money". Everyone that strives to just make money is usually broke. If you desire to earn a huge income so that you can change your life and the lives of others, then success is inevitable.

If you have a fear of closing, then you have to develop within you the ability to overcome that fear by developing

Are You a Member of the Fastest Growing Success & Motivation Club?
Check It Out Now! – www.LifestyleFreedomClub.com
17 Highly Controversial Motivational Teachings FREE ($497 value)

yourself. Without your belief structure, you can learn every how-to in the world of sales and still not succeed. I have outsold numerous so-called experts and coaches in the speaking world and online. It wasn't because I had any type of advantage that they didn't have. Let me explain something to you. Focus on this. I outsold them, because I out-believed them.

I absolutely believe in my products and services, which is self-development, motivation, success strategies, internet lead generation, and marketing strategies. I absolutely believe that my products and services will change people's lives, empower them, and equip them to fulfill their goals and dreams in life. It is my foundational belief in my products and services that empowers me to overcome the fear of closing and outsell nearly everyone else in the industry.

Strategy #1 Champion Tip: "Develop yourself and build your belief to overcome the fear of closing"

Strategy #2: Always Be Opening

I want you to lose the mindset of "Always Be Closing." That's ridiculous! I know that you are saying, "John, what are you talking about? You're losing your mind." Yes, I lost my mind over 18 years ago and gained the mind of a champion. See, the average mind, which includes the average mind of the average salesperson, never succeeds. You must lose your mind and gain the mind of someone that has achieved what you want to achieve in order to succeed. On a serious side note - Don't take direction from anyone that hasn't done what you want to do in life.

Over a seven-year period, I built a direct sales organization to over 25,000 reps in 10 countries. I know how to close. I know how to make people take action. I know how to transfer property that I have to them for them to own and become a long-term customer. That's why I have earned the right to teach you closing strategies. Once again, don't take

Are You a Member of the Fastest Growing Success & Motivation Club?
Check It Out Now! – www.LifestyleFreedomClub.com
17 Highly Controversial Motivational Teachings FREE *($497 value)*

direction from someone that hasn't done what you want to do in life. Okay, back to this teaching...

Lose that mindset of "Always Be Closing" and never find it again. What I want you to gain is this mindset of "Always Be Opening." I prefer to call a sales presentation the sales arena, because it's a sport - the sport of sales and marketing. You are preparing to win the sport so why would you use the negative terms like "always be closing". Think about the last time you went to a football game or watched any type of sports on television. Weren't the athletes fired up to win? They didn't go into the game with a negative mindset. It's the same in the sales arena. You have to look forward to the presentation and enter the arena with a positive mindset and outlook on the situation.

How good will it feel when you walk into your next sales presentation and shake the potential customer's hand with the mindset that you will know this person long-term. You believe that you will close the sale, but more importantly you

Are You a Member of the Fastest Growing Success & Motivation Club?
Check It Out Now! – www.LifestyleFreedomClub.com
17 Highly Controversial Motivational Teachings FREE *($497 value)*

will open up a life-changing relationship. Even if the

product that you're marketing (e.g., insurance, real estate,

products, services) is not for this specific individual right now,

you have opened up a long-term relationship. You're creating a

new contact and increasing your mastermind team. Right now, I

want you to think about these three words: Your Best Friend.

Who is your best friend? Can you see his or her face in

your mind? Now, just think at one time your best friend was a

stranger. You had no idea who they were or that they would

eventually be your best friend. At one point in time, you

opened up a relationship with them built upon trust. You

acknowledge and respect their opinion. That's exactly what

you're looking to do every time you sit down with someone in a

sales arena. You want to open a relationship. I'm not going to

promise that every single person that you meet during a sales

presentation will be your best friend or even someone that you

want on your mastermind team, but it's important that you

Are You a Member of the Fastest Growing Success & Motivation Club?
Check It Out Now! – www.LifestyleFreedomClub.com
17 Highly Controversial Motivational Teachings FREE *($497 value)*

enter that room with the "Always Be Opening" mindset no matter the person.

Just like when you open a window in your home and you let fresh air come in. I'm blessed to live in the Palm Beaches of South Florida. I open my living room door and the beautifully fresh air of south Florida blows in off the golf course. Any cobwebs, dust or dirt gets blown right out the door due to the cross ventilation from the front to the back of the house. It's the same with your sales presentation. You open that door to greet your potential client with an always be opening mindset and all of the prejudgment and misconceptions go right out the window. Just imagine that the person could be your next best friend so treat them with that courtesy and kindness.

I have hundreds of thousands of students all over the world, and I always try to treat everyone of them like friend of mine. I will do whatever it takes to maintain our relationship and over-deliver. My mindset is under-promise and over-deliver. With an always be opening mindset, I will give you

Are You a Member of the Fastest Growing Success & Motivation Club?
Check It Out Now! – www.LifestyleFreedomClub.com
17 Highly Controversial Motivational Teachings FREE *($497 value)*

whatever I can to empower you to achieve greatness and go to the next level.

Why is the "Always Be Opening" so important? Let me ask you that question. Do you want to be closed? Do enjoy the feeling that you get from a pushy sales person that is just trying to close you? Of course, you don't like that kind of treatment. If you don't like it, then why would you think that your potential business clients would like it? Instead, create a comfortable atmosphere and keep the "Always Be Opening" mindset. You will notice that your demeanor as well as the demeanor of your potential business partner will radically change.

Here's a great example. Let's say that you're a realtor. You show someone a home, but the home is not for that person. Two years later, they're back in the market for a home or have a friend looking for a home. Guess what? They call you. Why? Because you they remembered how you treated them. You had an open mindset and were looking to build a long-term relationship. Although, you didn't sell the house the

Are You a Member of the Fastest Growing Success & Motivation Club?
Check It Out Now! - www.LifestyleFreedomClub.com
17 Highly Controversial Motivational Teachings FREE ($497 value)

first time, you created a lasting bond with that person.

Your level of confidence stuck out to that person and they want to work with you again. Just think about having hundreds of people that ultimately come back to you or refer others to you, because of your very first sales presentation with them. It's realistic and completely possible for that to happen if you have the "Always Be Opening" mindset.

Strategy #2 Champion Tip: It's not "Always Be Closing". Lose that mindset and gain the champion mindset of "Always Be Opening".

Are You a Member of the Fastest Growing Success & Motivation Club?
Check It Out Now! – www.LifestyleFreedomClub.com
17 Highly Controversial Motivational Teachings FREE ($497 value)

Strategy #3: Never Prejudge

Let me share with you what the word prejudge means. Prejudge means making a mental decision prior to even engaging in a sales conversation or presentation. In your mind, you're already saying "You know what? This person doesn't have what it takes to invest in this home. This person doesn't have what it takes to invest in this network marketing opportunity. This person doesn't have what it takes to invest in this product or service." Never prejudge a potential client, customer, or prospect. This will be one of the worst mistakes that you make in your career!

Remember, I was never prospected for the industry of network marketing. No one ever prospected me. I was a stuttering twenty-four year old kid from Yonkers, New York that was simply not attractive to the average business builder. Here's the kicker...If someone would have prospected that stuttering kid, they would have earned over $1.1 million off the business that I built. I learned the industry, and I was looking

Are You a Member of the Fastest Growing Success & Motivation Club?
Check It Out Now! - www.LifestyleFreedomClub.com
17 Highly Controversial Motivational Teachings FREE ($497 value)

but no one ever approached me and gave me a chance to show my potential. Please don't e-mail me and prospect me now, I earned my financial freedom many years ago and retired from network marketing. I still get prospected several times a day, but my answer will ALWAYS be no. Why? Because I respect the fact that many of my students are involved with various companies and I would never jeopardize those relationships by joining any company.

Back to the topic...people prejudged me. They looked at me and saw a 24-year old stuttering kid that worked for his successful family business and had a good education. They assumed that I was completely content with my great level of success. That mindset cost numerous people millions -- literally over a million dollars. What they didn't see was that I was tired of working around the clock and was actively looking for another way of achieving financial freedom. I was hungry for change!

Think about it for a second. I lived in Yonkers, New York. I was often in Manhattan or Long Island. These are very heavily populated areas yet no one, no one, no one (I'm not stuttering) – NO ONE ever walked up to me and said, "By any chance are you looking to earn extra income? Do you love what you're doing? Do you want to be free?" Instead, people prejudged me. They walked by me every single day. It was definitely their loss!

Never prejudge. You must internalize this by saying to yourself, "I will NEVER prejudge someone in my business." You never know where someone's coming from. Don't judge them by their dress, by the car they drive or where they live. You never know what's going on inside their mind. Most people who you think have money don't have it, and those you think that don't have it, have tons of it.

When you meet a potential client, have an open mind. This was one strategy that catapulted my level of success. I treated every single person that I showed my business presentation to like they were my next top business partner. When you walk into a sales presentation and you're already

Are You a Member of the Fastest Growing Success & Motivation Club?
Check It Out Now! – www.LifestyleFreedomClub.com
17 Highly Controversial Motivational Teachings FREE *($497 value)*

saying to yourself, "I don't think this person has what it takes to invest in my product. I don't think this person has what it takes to get involved in this business", you are wasting your time. I don't care what you are selling - alarm systems, high-end art, furniture, kitchen cabinets, real estate, insurance, etc. If you prejudge that person before you even begin your business presentation, you are setting yourself up for failure.

Instead, enter the sales presentation saying to yourself, "I will show my product/business the exact same way to everyone with the belief that this person will become a customer of mine long-term." Once again, you're walking in with the "Always Be Opening" mind set. I'm opening up a new relationship. I'm not prejudging this potential client, customer, prospect, etc. Your mindset going into it will allow you to do a better presentation, and allow your excitement, enthusiasm, belief, conviction, and commitment to flow through. That's what people buy! They buy who you are. They physically buy your product, but they were sold on you.

If you're in one-on-one sales or if you're in network marketing, the potential client buys into you. They have to believe in you. If you walk in with a mindset of "I don't believe this person has what it takes to invest in this product or service", then they're going to feel that. They'll feel your non-belief. I love walking into some of the snooty shopping areas of Palm Beach in my gym clothes. If the sales person judges me on my clothing and gives me an attitude, then I walk right out the door. I refuse to sow my money into bad ground. In other words, I ain't giving my money to someone that treats me like garbage. That's exactly what your potential client will be thinking in their minds too if you prejudge them. Don't fool yourself to think that they won't know. They will notice the minute that you walk into the room. They will feel your non-belief in them, and that will dramatically cut your closing ratio down by 80 percent.

As I'm writing this I'm in beat up sneakers, my workout tank top and my workout pants. If you looked at me during the

Are You a Member of the Fastest Growing Success & Motivation Club?
Check It Out Now! – www.LifestyleFreedomClub.com
17 Highly Controversial Motivational Teachings FREE *($497 value)*

day, you'd walk right by me and say, oh, "Who is he? He doesn't have a job. Only a loser walks around in the middle afternoon with a hat on and unshaven." You are probably smirking right now, because you know that you have prejudged someone that looks exactly like that for your own business. Little do most people know, I can walk around like that in the middle of the afternoon, because I am free to do what I want, when I want and with who I want to do it with. That's far from being a loser! A prejudging mindset backed up with assumptions will cost you millions.

Allow EVERYONE the opportunity to own and take advantage of your exclusive offer to own your products. Enter every sales presentation with the belief that the person in front of you is your next big sale. I believe everyone has a champion inside them. Remember who I was and where I came from. No one ever prospected me. I had to answer an ad to get involved in network marketing and earn a million dollars. Isn't that incredible? No one gave me a chance. Don't you fall into that same trap of judging people. An open mind leads to a bountiful harvest!

Strategy #3 Champion Tip: NEVER prejudge or assume a potential client, a customer or prospect will not be able to afford or need your product.

Are You a Member of the Fastest Growing Success & Motivation Club?
Check It Out Now! – www.LifestyleFreedomClub.com
17 Highly Controversial Motivational Teachings FREE *($497 value)*

Strategy #4: Dress for Success

You know as well as I do that you feel better when you take a physical shower. Think about it. When you come home from the gym or work, there's nothing like taking a nice hot shower. For me, it's cutting the lawn. I have a pool in my backyard, and when the landscapers from our home owner's association come into my backyard, they blow grass into the pool. I am a maniac about my pool. I simply couldn't take it anymore so I posted a sign in Spanish that said "Stop. Do Not Cut the Grass!"

Now, I cut my own lawn, and there's never any grass in the pool. My friend, Bob, assists me with the lawn and when I'm finished I am sweaty. My wife, Christie, says that I smell like a little stinky kid that just came off the playground and pretty much demands that I take a shower right away. The refreshing shower washes away all the dirt, grim and most of all the smell from the hard work.

On the other hand, when you see me speak live, I am

always dressed sharp. People say, "John, you are always dressed to the ultimate. You are always one of the sharpest looking speakers or presenters". Absolutely! I believe in dressing for success. I completely disagree when people say, "Well, you don't need to dress like that to be successful". Everybody has a right to their own opinion, but I believe a major strategy for success is to dress the role. Can you imagine if I just came in from cutting the yard in my old shorts, tank top and hat smelling all gross and went straight to a seminar to speak? That's just simply absurd, right? Yet, many so-called sales experts enter the sales arena looking almost as bad.

Clean up your act. Men, go out and invest in some sharp ties. Buy some shirts with cufflinks. At the recommendation of one of my billionaire friends, I now get my nails manicured. Notice, I said BILLIONAIRE. If it works for him, then it will work for me too! Whether you believe it or not, people notice. The first impression is the most important

Are You a Member of the Fastest Growing Success & Motivation Club?
Check It Out Now! - www.LifestyleFreedomClub.com
17 Highly Controversial Motivational Teachings FREE ($497 value)

impression. I usually let my wife handle the women's issues with dressing for success but let me talk to the ladies for just a second. I will put this gently...You don't have to bare all of your assets to make a sale. I didn't say it. I'm just reiterating what my wife says, and I agree with her. Whether you are a man or a woman, make sure that you dress appropriately when you are in the sales arena. It will definitely have an effect on your sales presentation.

I disagree with a coach, who teaches success principles, and they look slothful. They don't look cleaned up. They're half asleep when they are talking to you, their clothes are wrinkled, and they are not dressed as a champion. It disgusts me when I see someone like that on stage trying to coach other people on success. Look at someone like Donald Trump. Donald Trump has a great wardrobe. You may not like what he says, but you can't dispute the fact that he is always dressed to the nines. Don't try to make the excuse that you can't afford his clothes. It's not expensive to look

Are You a Member of the Fastest Growing Success & Motivation Club?
Check It Out Now! – www.LifestyleFreedomClub.com
17 Highly Controversial Motivational Teachings FREE ($497 value)

professional.

When you walk into a presentation, the first thing people notice is how you look. They notice if your hair is a mess or if you are not clean-shaven as a man, or if you are wearing a suit that is too short or if you just threw on some jeans instead of dress slacks. Being dressed professionally not only influences your potential business partner, but it also gives you more confidence. When you clean up, you feel better. If you don't believe that, then don't take a shower for two weeks and see how you feel. With that said, why would you walk into a business event where you can market your product or services and you do not look like a champion? You don't look like who you know you want to be.

Make a decision today. Implement this strategy. For realtors or anyone that uses their automobiles to transport clients, make sure that your car isn't a pigpen. If a potential buyer gets in your car and there's garbage in the floorboards and it smells like three day old McDonald's food, I doubt that

Are You a Member of the Fastest Growing Success & Motivation Club?
Check It Out Now! – www.LifestyleFreedomClub.com
17 Highly Controversial Motivational Teachings FREE ($497 value)

they will want to book another appointment with you.

They simply can't get past your trashy car long enough to think about buying a house. I'm not saying that you have to drive a Mercedes, but your automobile does have to be clean so that your client is comfortable when they get in. I believe in cleanliness. I believe in excellence. I believe you should act and believe who you are.

Personal responsibility is the key. If someone is lazy and slothful, then they probably dress like a slob. If you consider yourself a business professional, then simply dress the role.

Strategy #4 Champion Tip: Dress for success. Feel good about the way that you look when you present your business or product to a potential customer.

Strategy #5: Always Be Early

I refuse to wait around on someone that is late.

Always be early! Pause there for a second, because I know that you're saying, "John, always be early? That's a strategy? What do you mean? I know I should be early." The keywords in that statement are I KNOW. I want you to make a mental note right now and take a look at the last ten sales presentations that you did. Were you early, were you late, or did you walk in at the same time as your prospect?

I can almost guarantee you that the times you were early, your closing ratio had a higher percentage. Why? When you walk into the sales arena and you're there first, the potential customer sits down and it's your territory. You own it, because you were there first. You have also had the opportunity to calm your nerves and build your confidence before the person arrives.

You're going to meet someone at a neutral location. Let's say you meet them at a local restaurant to sit down with

Are You a Member of the Fastest Growing Success & Motivation Club?
Check It Out Now! – www.LifestyleFreedomClub.com
17 Highly Controversial Motivational Teachings FREE ($497 value)

them and share your business, product, etc. You get there first so they are entering your arena. It's just a mental mindset. Now, think about it this way. The prospect is sitting there waiting for you. I bet you can almost feel your stomach turning flips as you imagine walking up to the table knowing that they have been waiting on you.

When you are late, the person that has been waiting on you has already likely made up his mind about what you are about to offer him and the answer is simply no thanks. After all, if you can't be on time for an appointment that was scheduled last week, then how on Earth will this person be able to depend on you if they invest in your product? If you are late, then you might as well just reschedule or call off the appointment all together. It's over! I don't care if you disagree with me, it's the truth and you know it.

My original mentor that mentored me over 18 years ago had earned over $30 million dollars at that point in his life. When he introduced someone to his business in direct sales, if

Are You a Member of the Fastest Growing Success & Motivation Club?
Check It Out Now! – www.LifestyleFreedomClub.com
17 Highly Controversial Motivational Teachings FREE ($497 value)

they were one minute late, he wouldn't show them the business. He would say, "Respect my time. I was here at 1:30. You showed up 1:31. Reschedule."

You're probably saying, "John, I can't do that!" Yes you can. Make a decision. I did. I refuse to let anyone waste a second of my time.

When I was building my business and conducted hotel presentations for business overviews, I started promptly at 7:35pm. The doors were actually locked at that time, and no one else was allowed to enter the presentation. One thing that aggravates me and upsets me to no end is when someone schedules a presentation that is supposed to start at 7:30pm and twenty minutes later they're still waiting for that one person to show up.

Respect the people who are there on time and get started on time. Don't worry about those people that are late for a business or product that you're sharing. Instead, focus on the people who are on time. They want to hear your

Are You a Member of the Fastest Growing Success & Motivation Club?
Check It Out Now! - www.LifestyleFreedomClub.com
17 Highly Controversial Motivational Teachings FREE *($497 value)*

presentation, need it and are serious about investing in it. NEVER start a business presentation late. Always be there early and start on time. The key is to always be there before your potential client.

Show respect for your client's schedule. My mentor said, "Look, if this person doesn't respect me enough to be here on time for the presentation that we set up, then I'm not going to show it. He must reschedule." People know I'm like that too. I'm known for always being on time for my appointments or always early. All of my coaching clients know. They don't even have to look at the phone when I call them. If I'm scheduled to call you at 2:00pm on Friday, then you can bet your last dollar that between 1:58pm and 2:00pm, that phone will jingle and John Di Lemme will be there to mentor you and coach you. I am always a few minutes early.

Here's another inside tip for you. In a restaurant setting, always drink water. Why? Coffee and soda give you bad breath. Remember, you are being judged on every aspect of

Are You a Member of the Fastest Growing Success & Motivation Club?
Check It Out Now! – www.LifestyleFreedomClub.com
17 Highly Controversial Motivational Teachings FREE ($497 value)

your presentation. I also suggest that you never drink alcohol at a sales presentation. It's unprofessional in my opinion. Drink water and that will be one less thing to worry about.

If you don't agree with this, that's fine. Just continue to lose sales. I'm giving you tips about the subconscious mind of your potential client. If you show up late drinking a cup of coffee, sweating, running behind schedule, looking like a slob, why should anyone buy from you? Think about that. Show up early. Dress professionally. Drink a glass of water. Be relaxed and then go for it. Get laser-focused and open up a brand new relationship.

Strategy #5 Champion Tip: Always be early. Respect your potential client's time and put yourself to ease before the sales presentation.

Are You a Member of the Fastest Growing Success & Motivation Club?
Check It Out Now! – www.LifestyleFreedomClub.com
17 Highly Controversial Motivational Teachings FREE *($497 value)*

Strategy #6: Grab a Pen that Writes

When I speak, I always say, "Grab a pen that writes." Make sure that you have an extra pen with you and even an extra notepad especially for those of you that are speakers and hosting your own events. When I speak, I always have at least twenty-five pens in my bag. Why? Just in case someone doesn't have a pen. I want to keep them engaged in the presentation.

When you are presenting to someone with nothing to write with or nothing to write on, it's great to be able to hand them a pen and a piece of paper or a notepad. It works even for those in real estate. If you are out showing a home, you can give your potential buyer the opportunity to take notes about what they like best about the house and write down questions that they may have for you after the showing.

When you give somebody the opportunity to write down any question, concern, or objection that means you are opening up the door. You are not trying to hide something. It

Are You a Member of the Fastest Growing Success & Motivation Club?
Check It Out Now! – www.LifestyleFreedomClub.com
17 Highly Controversial Motivational Teachings FREE ($497 value)

goes back to the foundation that you have an ethical, moral product. So, when you give someone a piece of paper and a pen, guess what? It shows that you are confident enough and you believe in your product or service so much that when you conclude your presentation, you feel comfortable and you are looking forward to answer any questions or concerns that they may have. That goes back to self-belief. Fear of success gets replaced with belief in yourself and your product/business.

I can see so many people at events saying, "Man, I wished I had a pen. I wanted to write that down. I forgot what you said." If this is you, then you have to get focused. You can't afford to miss an opportunity to take notes or write down important information that you know that you won't remember later. It's not only common sense, but a simple business strategy that will increase your sales ratio.

Always have a pen and paper. Consider those things part of your "sales uniform". Wouldn't a football player look foolish going to play a game without his helmet or a hockey

Are You a Member of the Fastest Growing Success & Motivation Club?
Check It Out Now! – www.LifestyleFreedomClub.com
17 Highly Controversial Motivational Teachings FREE ($497 value)

player being on the ice without his hockey stick? It's basic equipment for the sport of sales and marketing.

Strategy #6 Champion Tip: Always have a pen and notepad handy to give to the potential client and advise them to write down their questions or concerns about your product.

Are You a Member of the Fastest Growing Success & Motivation Club?
Check It Out Now! – www.LifestyleFreedomClub.com
17 Highly Controversial Motivational Teachings FREE ($497 value)

Strategy #7: The Power of Visualization

You all have heard it, but I'm going to share with you exactly how to do it and experience the power of visualization. You must visualize closing the sale and opening up relationships. Yes, I use the word closing. As you know from strategy number two, I don't have a closing mindset. However, your goal is still to close the sale after your presentation as well as open up relationships. The key is to see yourself doing it.

This is a strategy of all top salespeople. When I was in sales full-time, I went to every presentation with the paperwork and contract filled out prior to going to the presentation. I had everything filled out - all the boxes checked, the date of the presentation, name of the client, etc. The only thing that I needed was the person's signature. Before the presentation, I visualized myself delivering an excellent presentation and the person signing the paperwork.

I want you to do it right now. You're reading this, because you're a champion and you want to earn heavy six and

Are You a Member of the Fastest Growing Success & Motivation Club?
Check It Out Now! - www.LifestyleFreedomClub.com
17 Highly Controversial Motivational Teachings FREE ($497 value)

seven figures year-end in sales, correct? If so, flip down your laptop computer so you're not checking your email, turn your cell phone off, and lower the sound that you have playing in the background.

Now, visualize the exact contract, agreement or paperwork that you need to get paid your commission. I want you to visualize it. Your eyes are closed. The paperwork is in your hand. I want you to literally visualize that paperwork in your client's hand and imagine the client sticking her hand out saying, "I'm so excited that you shared your business with me. Thank you so very much! Here's the signed contract." Then see yourself saying back to her, "I look forward to building a long, prosperous business relationship with you."

How does that feel? Can you imagine if you did that every single time before you enter a sales presentation? You literally have to visualize the paperwork being exchanged, the acceptance of the contract, the acceptance of the agreement, and/or the transfer of the product from you to them. It truly

Are You a Member of the Fastest Growing Success & Motivation Club?
Check It Out Now! – www.LifestyleFreedomClub.com
17 Highly Controversial Motivational Teachings FREE ($497 value)

works. You have to talk yourself through the process. Self-talk is very important. Build up your self-belief by saying, "I am a closer, I am opening new relationships. Today is the day I will open five new relationships. Today is the day the number one sale I've ever done in my sales career will manifest. Today is the best day of my life." You have to tell yourself that you are worthy of that type of success and believe it.

Let's say that you're selling insurance and you open up the door of a potential client. You have to visualize yourself leaving with the signed insurance forms. Always have the agreement entirely filled out. Here's the most important part...Always use a yellow highlighter to highlight where they need to sign rather than using red pen to make an X before their signature. People don't like to sign contracts anyway so why would you use a big huge X red to mark the spot. It's so negative. Using a yellow highlighter is less intrusive and more reader friendly than a giant X.

Also, never be fumbling around. When a person is ready to do the deal, you need to be ready to authorize the paperwork. You don't need to be filling out their name, address, and all that stuff that you could have done before hand. Do everything you can prior to entering the sales arena. Prepare to close the deal. Flip the paperwork around, slide it across the table to the buyer, review the details and explain to him that you need his signature on the highlighted areas. Use positive keywords like authorize, endorse, agree, and invest. Show the buyer that you are serious about your business and building a relationship with them.

I challenged you to test this for 90 days. Test out the power of visualization. As you're driving, obviously you can't close your eyes, but speak the words. "Today is the day that my client is authorizing the paperwork to own the $1 million piece of real estate that I am marketing to him. Today is the day that he will take ownership of the million dollar piece of real estate that I am listing." How much would those positive words and

Are You a Member of the Fastest Growing Success & Motivation Club?
Check It Out Now! – www.LifestyleFreedomClub.com
17 Highly Controversial Motivational Teachings FREE *($497 value)*

visualization change your sales revenues? The power of visualization is unbelievable. In other words, not believable to the average person, but believable to the champion, and that's what you are. I guarantee this will close your sales. Test it for 90 days and email me with your results at John@LifestyleFreedomClub.com.

Strategy # 7 Champion Tip: Invest time in the power of visualization. Visualize the paperwork being completed and endorsed by your new client. Remember to use a yellow highlighter instead of a red pen. Simple strategies yield great results.

Are You a Member of the Fastest Growing Success & Motivation Club?
Check It Out Now! – www.LifestyleFreedomClub.com
17 Highly Controversial Motivational Teachings FREE *($497 value)*

Strategy #8: Shotgun Versus Sniper

No, I'm not talking about the military. Listen up...Everyone walks into sales presentations like a shotgun. They try to blow up their prospects with tons of information, details, statistics and other useless knowledge. The presentation is not structured and takes too much time. The tactic is to confuse them to close them. Unfortunately, there are many sales managers that teach this tactic and it's completely unethical. I can guarantee you that anyone that teaches or uses that type of closing strategy does not have long-lasting, profitable relationships.

Instead, be a sniper during your presentation. Know exactly what you need to cover briefly in order to close the sale and open the relationship. Share with them just enough to pique their interest and generate questions. If you expect to handle every objection and every concern during your presentation, you are wasting your time. You can handle the majority of them, but there's simply no way that you will be able to tackle every question and concern during the initial presentation.

Unlike a shotgun, a sniper will focus in and take one shot at their target. No, I'm not saying to annihilate your customer, but you have to be as focused as a sniper on your ultimate goal. Your target is to close every sale and open up a long-term prosperous relationship. You don't want to just confuse the daylights out of the person, close the sale and move on to the next victim. Once again, that's unethical and no way to build a prosperous business.

Here's a bonus for you. Most sales presentations should be limited to one hour. Yes, that's only 60 minutes in which you will present your business/product for the first 30 minutes. The remaining 30 minutes will be completely devoted to any questions or concerns voiced by your customer. After you finish your presentation, ask them, "What did you like best about it?" This empowers the person to speak positively about

Are You a Member of the Fastest Growing Success & Motivation Club?
Check It Out Now! - www.LifestyleFreedomClub.com
17 Highly Controversial Motivational Teachings FREE ($497 value)

your presentation. This is their time so just let them talk and ask questions. You basically shut-up and listen at this point.

Let's say for real estate, the time of the showing will vary due to the factors involved in showing the home, but still don't drag out the showing. Be prompt and courteous of the buyer's time. After the showing, ask the buyer, "What did you like best about the house?" Of course, they will tell you the positive side of things after the question. This question will lead into them telling you what they didn't like about the house such as they really wanted a view of the ocean. You still have the upper hand in this situation, because you can respond with something like, "Excellent! As a matter of fact, I have three more homes with that a view of the ocean that I can show to you tomorrow." Even though that house wasn't for the buyer, you listened and focused in on the buyer's need to have the opportunity to show them a few other properties.

I know that I can sell product that I believe in, and I mean anything - real estate, high-end cars, furniture, nutrition,

Are You a Member of the Fastest Growing Success & Motivation Club?
Check It Out Now! - www.LifestyleFreedomClub.com
17 Highly Controversial Motivational Teachings FREE ($497 value)

kitchen cabinets, anything under the sun, etc. Give me a sales presentation to do, and I will outsell the number one salesman, I guarantee it. It's not based on my knowledge of the product. The end result of the sale is all about my belief in myself, the product and the sniper sales process. I'm confident that I can show the plan, handle the objections, close the sale and open a relationship with the prospect. It's not difficult. You just have to be laser-focused!

That's why most salespeople never achieve any success, because they never get to the point. They just go on and on and on and on and on and on. Excuse my language, but I call it diarrhea of the mouth. By the time the salesperson is finished, the client has already decided not to invest in the product. All that useless information is highly ineffective and completely unnecessary.

You have to out-listen your competition. Since you know that most sales professionals talk too much, just make the decision to out-listen them. Listen to that potential client's

Are You a Member of the Fastest Growing Success & Motivation Club?
Check It Out Now! - www.LifestyleFreedomClub.com
17 Highly Controversial Motivational Teachings FREE ($497 value)

questions and concerns like you are being told the biggest secret in the world. You have to have ears like Dumbo tuned into every word that they are saying. Of course, your ultimate goal is to outsell your competition, but you have to out-listen first and then your sales will skyrocket.

Strategy #8 Champion Tip: Become a sniper and focus on your target. Out-listen to outsell your competition.

Strategy #9: An Offensive Mindset Versus a Defensive Mindset

When you enter the sales arena, you must have an offensive mindset knowing that you're going to win the game. You have to be confident in your abilities to close the sale and open the relationship. Your potential business client will take notice of your offensive mindset the minute you enter the room. It will be evident that you believe in yourself and your business so much that you do not waiver when answering their questions or handling their objections.

Too many people in the sales process are worried about everything when they enter the room – "Will the client think my product is too expensive? Are they going to hate my presentation?" Stop it! Lose that mindset. If you're questioning the value of what you are selling and you have to constantly defend it, then stop selling it. You have to fully believe in what you sell. That's why I can sell personal self-development, I love it and I believe in it. It's my product, and I use it daily.

Allowing yourself to become defensive when faced with

Are You a Member of the Fastest Growing Success & Motivation Club?
Check It Out Now! – www.LifestyleFreedomClub.com
17 Highly Controversial Motivational Teachings FREE ($497 value)

objections, questions, or concerns in the sales process will decrease the likelihood that you will close the sale or open a relationship. You should embrace questions and concerns. Think about the last big investment that you made. Did you have questions and concerns? Of course, you did. It would be foolish not to ask questions or raise objections about a product or service that you are going to invest your money in. If you expect the questions and handle them with an offensive mindset, then your potential client will acknowledge that and feel comfortable doing business with you.

There are many people that I meet at seminars, but many of them never "do business" with me that particular day. I don't huff and puff about their decision not to invest in my products and services. That's fine, because I believe in creating long-term relationships. I believe in the near future, they will invest in one of my product or services. Maybe they become a member of the Lifestyle Freedom Club, attend a boot camp or hire me to do a motivational seminar for their company. I

Are You a Member of the Fastest Growing Success & Motivation Club?
Check It Out Now! - www.LifestyleFreedomClub.com
17 Highly Controversial Motivational Teachings FREE ($497 value)

handled that initial rejection of my products and services appropriately and welcomed them to tie into my emails, tele-classes, etc., which led to their investment at a later date. Creating long-term relationships despite not closing that initial sale is a huge part of maintaining an offensive mindset.

What if I would have responded with a defensive mindset? "I don't need their money anyway. I would rather keep my products, because they aren't going to use them." The chances of that person tying into my company resources and investing at a later date just flew out the door. Who wants to do business with someone that gets so defensive over another person's decision not to do business at that time? More importantly, why would that person refer you to anyone else that is looking for the product/service that you have to offer with an attitude like that? For most people, it's easy to get hot under the collar when a buyer is talking bad about a business that you believe in, but always remember the importance of opening those relationships.

You can remain strong in your convictions about your business without completely ruining the sale. Just focus on the question or concern and address it with the reasons that you stand behind your product. You can even say something like, "That's an excellent question." If they say, it costs too much, then simply say, "I see you're concerned about value?" Instead of giving off the feeling that you think they are just being cheap. Strive to satisfy their questions with your belief. Remember, if you don't believe in what you are selling, then stop trying to sell it to others.

Strategy #9 Champion Tip: Maintain an offensive mindset that's full of energy, excitement, focus and strength. When questions arise, get excited. Stand behind your business product/services and allow your belief to drive you to handle all questions and concerns.

Are You a Member of the Fastest Growing Success & Motivation Club?
Check It Out Now! - www.LifestyleFreedomClub.com
17 Highly Controversial Motivational Teachings FREE ($497 value)

Strategy #10: Closing/Opening Words

When you show your sales presentation, never use the words "if" or "think." I hear so many people say, "If you like this product, you may want to think about getting a hold of it today. These words are deadly words. If and think are fear-based words that cause your potential buyer to question whether or not they really want to close the deal.

Instead, use words like "I believe" or "When you invest in the package" or "What did you like best about it?" Did you see the flip switch there? The language went from questioning the sale to empowering the buyer to invest in the product/services. Every word that you say during your presentation has to be focused on closing the sale and opening up the relationship.

These are the top four closing/opening phrases that you must use at the end of your presentation:

- Let's recap

- Let's summarize

- Let me tie it all together for you

- With that said, do you have any questions?

No, you don't use all of them at one time. You can just use one phrase to sum up your entire presentation for the customer.

Many of you have seen me use these same phrases in e-mails and at live events when I present my product offer from stage. It's a closing strategy that brings it all together. If you don't have a recap after your presentation, you often lose key points in the mix of things. It's also a great way to transition from your presentation to your close not matter what you are selling or who you are selling to.

I highly suggest that you record every single presentation that you do so you can listen to your words and hear what you sound like. You will be able to determine how effective you were in not only tying everything together, but also using positive keywords. Don't make it so obvious to the

Are You a Member of the Fastest Growing Success & Motivation Club?
Check It Out Now! – www.LifestyleFreedomClub.com
17 Highly Controversial Motivational Teachings FREE *($497 value)*

client that's listening. Just stick a recording in your briefcase so that you can hear yourself. Believe me. After you do this a few times, you will pick up on everything that you said that may have jeopardized your sale or relationship with the client.

Strategy #10: "With all that said, let's recap. Let's summarize. Let me tie it all together for you." You are preparing for your closing and confident in what you have just presented.

Strategy #11: The Opening Million Dollar Question

I've already shared a little bit of this strategy with you, and many of you have seen me teach this live at boot camps. It is so crucial. Close your sales presentation with an open ended, positive question. Let me break that down for you before I get to the million dollar question.

Open-ended means that you are stating a question in a way that it is going to encourage a full answer. You aren't going to allow your potential customer to get away with saying something like no, yes, uh-huh or any other answer that doesn't give the opportunity to know exactly what they are thinking about your product, service, business, etc. This type of question also clearly lets the business prospect know that you are finished with your presentation, and it's their turn to ask questions or voice concerns.

Let me give you a few examples for those of you that sell real estate: "John and Christie, what did you like best about the home?"

Do you see how that question empowers the buyer to not only answer the question fully, but also to focus on the positive things that they like about the house first? What you are doing is you are extracting, developing, and building from them a positive response. What if you would have said this instead: "John and Christie, what did you think about the home?"

That's a horrible question! Why? Because most people "think" negative. You never want to ask anyone what they "think" about your product, service, business or whatever your selling. Those are weak words and don't empower the buyer to do anything other than to complain.

After you ask the open-ended, positive question, you just listen to their response and then build off of that response to handle their questions and concerns. I already let the cat out of the bag in which it is likely obvious to you that the real million dollar closing question is "What did you like best about it?" You will just replace the "it" with whatever you are

Are You a Member of the Fastest Growing Success & Motivation Club?
Check It Out Now! – www.LifestyleFreedomClub.com
17 Highly Controversial Motivational Teachings FREE ($497 value)

selling.

The next few strategies are short and sweet and tie together so make sure that you are taking notes and not skipping ahead on the reading.

Strategy #11 Champion Tip: Always use open-ended positive questions at the end of your presentation to empower your buyer to answer the question fully and in a positive manner.

Are You a Member of the Fastest Growing Success & Motivation Club?
Check It Out Now! – www.LifestyleFreedomClub.com
17 Highly Controversial Motivational Teachings FREE ($497 value)

Strategy #12: You're Right About That

When the realtor that showed me the home that Christie and I currently live in asked me, "So, what do you like best about the house?" I actually said, "I absolutely love the view. I am so close to the course that I can actually chat with the golfers." We wanted a view where we could see the sunset. That was really important to us. I also liked the pool, but the view was the selling point. However, there were other things in the home that we didn't like, and we knew that we were going to have to remodel the majority of the house.

In my situation, I negotiated a great price with the realtor due to the fact that we did like something really great about house. But let me show you how the "You're right about that" strategy would have worked for the realtor. After I told the realtor my thoughts about the view, he should have said:

"John and Christie, you're absolutely right about that. That is a gorgeous view and the sunsets are absolutely spectacular."

Why would it benefit the realtor to make that

Are You a Member of the Fastest Growing Success & Motivation Club?
Check It Out Now! – www.LifestyleFreedomClub.com
17 Highly Controversial Motivational Teachings FREE *($497 value)*

statement during the sales process? He would have enhanced the one very thing that we absolutely loved about the house. Let me give you another example. You are in car sales and your buyer just drove the new BMW 5 series. You can tell that she absolutely loves the car, but has some price objections. After the test drive, you ask her "What do you like best about the car?" She says something like "I love the way that it drives." Your response begins with "You're right about that." Then you expound upon the unique driving style of the car and what she really likes best about it.

You see, we are moving through the successful sales process:

- Opening

- Presentation

- Asking, "What do you like best about it?"

- Listening to their answer

- Agreeing with the buyer with "You're right about that"

- Focusing on the strengths of the product, service, business, etc.

Are You a Member of the Fastest Growing Success & Motivation Club?
Check It Out Now! – www.LifestyleFreedomClub.com
17 Highly Controversial Motivational Teachings FREE ($497 value)

- Closing the sale with the paperwork that you have already prepared

- Ultimately, creating a long-term relationship

Strategy #12 Champion Tip: Use "You're right about that" enhance what the buyer really likes about the product.

Are You a Member of the Fastest Growing Success & Motivation Club?
Check It Out Now! - www.LifestyleFreedomClub.com
17 Highly Controversial Motivational Teachings FREE ($497 value)

Strategy #13: Actively Listening

Ninety-seven percent of people that are in sales and marketing simply do not listen to their buyer. They think they know everything about what the buyer wants. If they would simply listen to the buyer instead of talking, then they would really know what the buyer wanted and understand how they could close the sale for their product/service. Before I speak at an event, I will ask the promoter, "What do you believe the attendees need to hear to change their lives?" At that point, I shut-up and listen. By actively listening to the wants and needs of the attendees, my sales increase and I build relationships.

These are two powerful words: Shut-up and listen. After you ask your open-ended, positive closing questions, you have to be silent. The cool thing is that if you rearrange the letters in the word "silent", you will get "listen." Further proving that the two go hand-in-hand. When you are actively listening, you are focused. You are not distracted or multi-

Are You a Member of the Fastest Growing Success & Motivation Club?
Check It Out Now! – www.LifestyleFreedomClub.com
17 Highly Controversial Motivational Teachings FREE ($497 value)

tasking while your potential client is speaking. Multi-tasking equals multi-failing in this situation so don't do it. You have to respect the client's words and listen to what they really want in order to successfully close the sale and open a relationship.

Strategy #13 Champion Tip: Shut-up and listen to really hear the needs of your client and close the sale.

Are You a Member of the Fastest Growing Success & Motivation Club?
Check It Out Now! – www.LifestyleFreedomClub.com
17 Highly Controversial Motivational Teachings FREE ($497 value)

Strategy #14: Follow-Up

How do you close? Remember, not everybody makes a decision the first day. Many people want to wait and see if you are going be around six months from now. They want to be assured that you believe in your product/service so much that you are sticking it out for the long haul and would be there to support them if they invested in what you are offering. Your clients have every right to do that based on 97% of people in sales and marketing skipping from one product to the next.

So, how do you handle that type of situation? You follow-up and maintain contact with them. You likely have their email address, phone number and mailing address so just keep them posted on what you are doing. No, don't pester them. Just keep them in the loop. There's a lady that tried to sell my wife some cosmetics, but Christie just wasn't interested at the time. Since the initial presentation at the department store, the lady has mailed postcards to Christie to let her know about upcoming sales. She followed up with her after the initial presentation, and Christie has invested in the products from time to time.

Strategy #14 Champion Tip: Take the time to follow-up with your customer and prove to them that you believe in your product and you are dedicated to building your business.

Strategy #15: Take Follow-Up to the Next Level

Thank you cards. You must send out thank you cards. Preferably a handwritten thank you card instead of an e-card, because people get bombarded with e-mails. This is something that I do regularly in my business to thank people for their time and consideration. It's not enough to just sign your name to some random thank you card. Take just a few moments to actually write the person's name and a short blurb thanking them for their time, consideration or whatever it was that they did for you. You must do this even if the person did not invest in your product. Remember, the key is to build long-term relationships.

I also suggest that you go online and invest in a birthday card system. You can actually send birthday cards, thank you cards, and holiday cards to your entire database of clients. It's that little bit of extra that makes you extraordinary and stick out from your competition. Your clients remember these added touches when they are in the

Are You a Member of the Fastest Growing Success & Motivation Club?
Check It Out Now! – www.LifestyleFreedomClub.com
17 Highly Controversial Motivational Teachings FREE ($497 value)

market for your product or have a referral.

Strategy #15 Champion Tip: Send out thank you cards just to let your clients know that you really do appreciate the time that they invested with your business.

Are You a Member of the Fastest Growing Success & Motivation Club?
Check It Out Now! – www.LifestyleFreedomClub.com
17 Highly Controversial Motivational Teachings FREE *($497 value)*

Strategy #16: Become a Record Breaker

This is my favorite strategy, because I love to set goals and break records. It keeps me motivated and focused on achieving more than I have already accomplished. If you are a record breaker, then you can never become complacent.

What is your personal sales record? What is the most that you have ever earned in sales? Write it down right now. Now, what's your record breaking goal? Write that down. Also, write down when you want to accomplish that goal. Now, put that record breaking goal and the date in front of you so that you see it everyday. Let me give you the three steps that will guarantee that you will break the record.

First, you must know it in order to break it. Sales records are developed, recorded in the books and then broken. Someone in your sales organization, business or in the same industry is the top earner. Find out what their check is per month and set a goal to break it. I broke records in every single network marketing company that I was involved in.

Are You a Member of the Fastest Growing Success & Motivation Club?
Check It Out Now! – www.LifestyleFreedomClub.com
17 Highly Controversial Motivational Teachings FREE ($497 value)

How? I set the goal of being the top earner and the date of when I would achieve it. I got focused and did it!

If there's no one for you to compete with in your industry, then strive to beat your own personal record. What is your personal sales record? What's the most you ever earned? If you're an independent contractor, what's the highest 1099 filed? Find it out. Look at it, cross it out and commit to breaking that record. This works for anyone in sales and marketing.

Secondly, you must own it. Create a check of the exact amount that you want to earn by a certain date and put it somewhere so that you can see it everyday. One of my students wrote out a check for $7,000 and dated it three months out from that date. She posted a copy of that check everywhere so that she challenged herself everyday to break that record. She actually earned a check that was seventeen percent more than what the amount was on that check. Take action today and write down the exact amount you want earn 90 days from now.

Are You a Member of the Fastest Growing Success & Motivation Club?
Check It Out Now! - www.LifestyleFreedomClub.com
17 Highly Controversial Motivational Teachings FREE ($497 value)

Thirdly, understand that records are made to be broken. When Roger Bannister broke the four-minute mile, within the next three years over twenty other people did it too. What happened? Did legs and feet get different? No. The mind believed that it was possible. Because one person did it, everyone else knew it was possible. Well, guess what? You can do it too. Find out the record numbers in your company or within your own sales and commit to breaking them by a certain date. You can do it! Don't let any tell you that it's impossible.

I'm in full agreement with you that you CAN break records. There is no doubt about it! Just set the date and break the record. Go for it!

Strategy #16 Champion Tip: Determine the most that you've ever earned on one sale and strive to break the record. Write out a check with the date that you believe that you will break that record and put it in a place so that you see it every day.

Strategy #17: Commitment - Most People Quit. Will You?

Let's say that you are in real estate and you show a home to a couple in September 2008. They don't purchase the home from you, but you send a thank you card and keep them in the loop of your business. Three years later, they are looking to purchase another home. Most likely, the realtor that sold them a home quit, moved or changed phone numbers, but you have been dripping on them. Now, they are ready to upgrade. Maybe they purchased a townhouse for $150,000.00 from the first realtor. Now, they want to purchase an $800,000.00 home. They see the yearly refrigerator calendar that you mailed them during the holidays and called you to see property.

Isn't that awesome? That's what happens when you commit to opening up long-term relationships with clients. It actually happened with me and my current broker. I didn't use his services initially, but he kept sending me information and caught my eye with some of his promos. It was nearly four

Are You a Member of the Fastest Growing Success & Motivation Club?
Check It Out Now! – www.LifestyleFreedomClub.com
17 Highly Controversial Motivational Teachings FREE ($497 value)

years before I engaged in any type of business with him. I saw that he was committed to his business and believed that he would be just as committed to my business with him.

Are you committed? Will you quit? If you are going to quit in whatever product or service you are doing right now, just please quit now for the benefit of the other ethical, moral champions involved in sales and marketing. Please quit now and let those who have a right to earn huge income do it when they have an ethical and moral product and/or service. BUT if you are truly committed to the process, then take action and start implementing the strategies that you have learned in this book to radically increase your sales ration and open up hundreds of long-term relationships.

Strategy #17 Champion Tip: Stay committed and follow-up on the relationships that you have opened up. You will build trust with them through your commitment of opening up long-term relationships and earn the right to do business with them.

Are You a Member of the Fastest Growing Success & Motivation Club?
Check It Out Now! – www.LifestyleFreedomClub.com
17 Highly Controversial Motivational Teachings FREE ($497 value)

Conclusion

I have shared my most high-guarded sales strategies with you and I expect for you to learn them. Don't just let this book sit on your desk and become shelf help. Implement these strategies into your current sales presentations and watch your sales skyrocket. Remember, opening relationships is the key to long-term success. I want to hear your record-breaking sales testimonials so email me at John@ChampionsLiveFree.com.